Invaders and Settlers

Keith Dickson

Links to all SSU themes

Oxford University Press 1993

The publishers wish to thank the following for permission
to reproduce copyright material:

Front cover: British Museum; p.4 *top* John Brennan, *centre left*
Dorset Natural History and Archaeological Society, Dorset
County Museum, Dorchester; p.8 Colchester Museums; p.12
Bridgeman Art Library (Museum of Antiquities, Newcastle upon
Tyne); p.13 Aspect Picture Library; p.17 Archäologisches
Landesmuseum, Schleswig; p.20 National Museum,
Copenhagen; p.23 Werner Forman Archive; p.24 Ashmolean
Museum, Oxford; p.26 British Museum; pp.30 and 31 St.
Edmundsbury Borough Council and West Stow Anglo Saxon
Village; pp.32 and 33 British Museum; pp.36 and 37 British
Library; pp.38 and 39 Martin Chilmaid; pp.40, 44 and 45
British Library.

Illustrations by: Dick Barnard, Peter Dennis, Nick Hawken,
Richard Hook, John James, Chris Molan, Tony Morris and
Mike White.

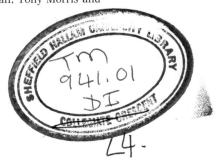

Oxford University Press, Walton Street, Oxford OX2 6DP

Oxford   New York   Toronto
Delhi   Bombay   Calcutta   Madras   Karachi
Kuala Lumpur   Singapore   Hong Kong   Tokyo
Nairobi   Dar es Salaam   Cape Town
Melbourne   Auckland   Madrid

and associated companies in
Berlin and *Ibadan*

Oxford is a trade mark of Oxford University Press

ISBN 0 19 917213 7

Typeset by Positif Press, Oxford
Printed in Hong Kong

Invaders Time Line

The Roman Invasion
A.D.43

Boudicca's Revolt
A.D.62

Hadrian's Wall
A.D.122

Anglo-Saxon raids
About A.D.350 – A.D.400

Viking raids
Started in A.D.787

Alfred the Great
A.D.871 – 901

**Viking Invasions and
Settlements
from A.D.850 onwards**

Contents

An exciting discovery

Stories may be about real people or fictional people.

Some people dig for clues under the ground.

They are called archaeologists.

Some of the objects that archaeologists find are very old.

They use the objects they find to try to work out what happened in the past.

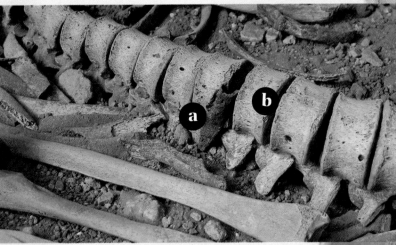

The objects in the photograph were found in a place where a group of Britons once lived.

Can you work out what **a** and **b** were? How did the archaeologists know these objects were old? How do you think the objects had got where they were found?

Bran's story will help you to answer the questions.

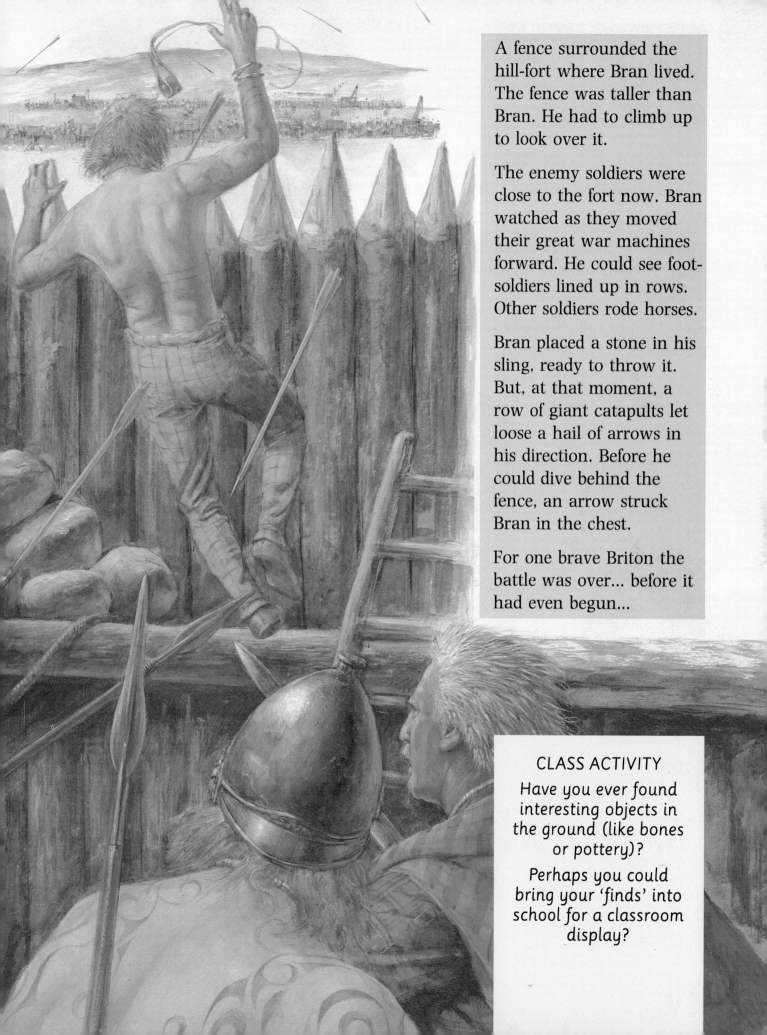

A fence surrounded the hill-fort where Bran lived. The fence was taller than Bran. He had to climb up to look over it.

The enemy soldiers were close to the fort now. Bran watched as they moved their great war machines forward. He could see foot-soldiers lined up in rows. Other soldiers rode horses.

Bran placed a stone in his sling, ready to throw it. But, at that moment, a row of giant catapults let loose a hail of arrows in his direction. Before he could dive behind the fence, an arrow struck Bran in the chest.

For one brave Briton the battle was over... before it had even begun...

CLASS ACTIVITY

Have you ever found interesting objects in the ground (like bones or pottery)?

Perhaps you could bring your 'finds' into school for a classroom display?

Views of the past

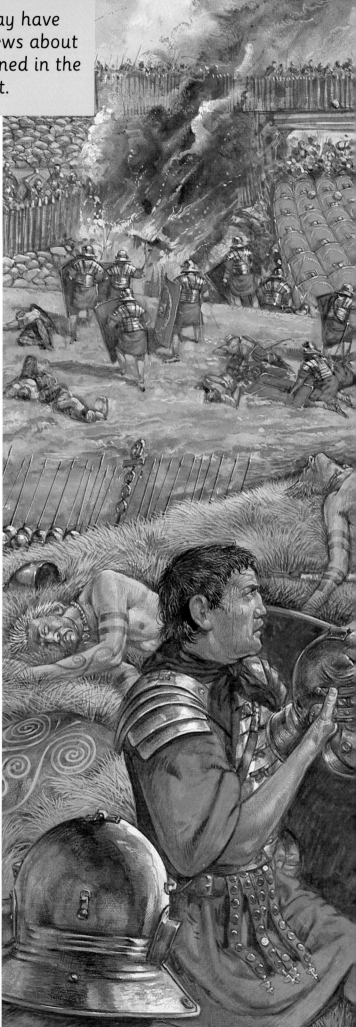

Some children have been looking at the picture on these pages.

The picture imagines what happened when Roman soldiers attacked Bran's hill-fort.

The children talked to one another about the things they could see.

Paul said:

The place where the Britons lived was like a castle.

Amy said:

And we know about one Briton who lived there. We know the story about Bran. Here is the fence he was standing behind.

Carl said:

I would like to make drawings of the different things people were throwing or firing.

Krishna said:

The Romans wore heavy armour and carried shields. This was to protect them in battle.

John said:

Yes... some have put their shields together. It looks like the roof of a building.

Dawn said:

The Roman soldiers have reached the entrance to the fort. I think they must have won the battle.

CLASS ACTIVITY

When the children looked at the picture, each of them noticed different things.

Make a list of five different things you can see in the picture.

Then show what you have written to your classmates.

Did different people see different things? Can you think why?

Did he fall or was he pushed?

The photograph below shows a tombstone. It marked the place where a Roman soldier was buried.

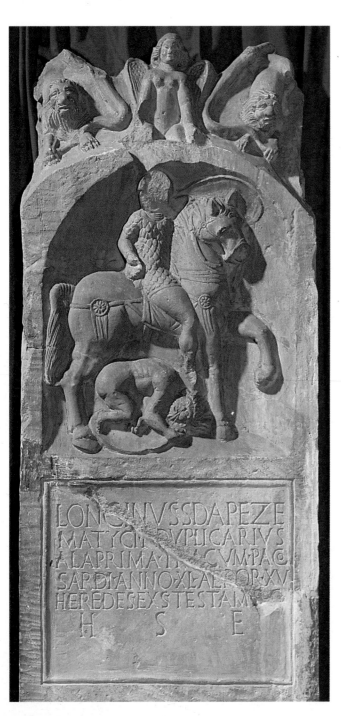

The writing carved on the stone is in a language called Latin.

It tells you:

1. The soldier's name was Longinus.

2. He was aged forty when he died.

3. He had been in the Roman army for fifteen years.

The tombstone can now be seen in Colchester Museum.

It was broken in different places when it was found.

It was lying on the ground face down.

Archaeologists cannot be sure whether the tombstone had fallen down, or been pushed over on purpose.

Now look closely at the photograph.

Which type of soldier was Longinus?

What did he wear and use to protect himself from his enemies?

Who do you think the man under his horse was meant to be?

What do you think had happened to the tombstone of Longinus?

Read pages 10 and 11 for more clues...

CLASS ACTIVITY

These Roman soldiers are travelling on foot and by horseback.

Find out more about Roman roads and travel.

Why did the Romans build roads?
What did their roads look like?
Which places did they link?
What other forms of transport were there?

Boudicca...
Warrior Queen

To understand a story
the events need to be
in the correct order.

This picture strip tells the story of Boudicca. Queen of the Britons.

Use the pictures to help you place these parts of the story in the correct order:

The Britons attacked Colchester.

Boudicca was whipped by Roman soldiers.

Boudicca poisoned herself.

The Britons revolted against Roman rule.

The Roman army defeated Boudicca's army.

The Britons paid taxes to the Romans.

1. Not everyone was happy to be ruled by the Romans...

2. Some Britons had to give up their land to the Romans...

3. Boudicca led many Britons in a revolt against Roman rule...

4. Boudicca's army set fire to buildings in Colchester...

5. A Roman army marched to do battle with Boudicca...

6. The Romans defeated Boudicca, who poisoned herself rather than be taken prisoner...

Now use the pictures to answer these WHY questions:

Why was the Roman army on the march? (Picture 5)

Why did Boudicca poison herself? (Picture 6)

Why was Boudicca whipped by Roman soldiers? (Picture 2)

Why did the Britons set fire to the temple in Colchester? (Pictures 1 and 4)

Why did the Roman army defeat Boudicca's army? (Pictures 5 and 6)

Why did the Britons revolt against Roman rule? (Pictures 1 and 2)

A hole in the wall

Clues can tell you about important events, as well as everyday ones.

Lucius the stonemason worked carefully. This was an important job. He did not want to make any mistakes.

The stonemason began with the Latin word for Emperor, IMPERATOR. He carved IMP for short.

Next came the Emperor's name, CAESAR TRAJAN HADRIAN AUGUSTUS.

After this, the stonemason carved another name, and a number, the SECOND LEGION AUGUSTA.

This was the name of the group of soldiers who had built the wall in which the stone was to fit.

But it would not be put in place on that day. The stonemason was tired. Evening was approaching. He would continue his work when daylight returned...

The object in this photograph was found where a Roman fort had once stood.

The fort had been built alongside a great wall known as Hadrian's Wall.

It gets its name from the Roman leader or Emperor called Hadrian.

Hadrian's Wall today

A warlike tribe called the Picts often attacked the land held by the Romans. The wall and fort helped defend it.

This picture imagines how Hadrian's Wall was built. What was the stonemason doing in this picture?

Now use the clues on these pages to say:

> what the letters LEGIIAVG meant,

> why the stonemason carved IMP and not IMPERATOR,

> why you think the stone was carved,

> where you think the stone was placed.

Check your last answer with the picture on page 15.

Defending the Roman Empire

Can you imagine what an attack on Hadrian's Wall was like?

There are word and picture clues on these pages to help you.

The sentences below tell the different parts of the story. But they are not in the correct order.

The sentry rushed down into the fort and sounded the alarm.

The sentry saw strangers approach the wall.

Soldiers marched from their fort to help those under attack.

Soldiers at the large fort nearby saw the warning.

A Roman soldier was on sentry duty above the gateway to the fort.

Another soldier lit the signal fire.

He could see they were carrying weapons.

14

First, put the sentences in the order in which they happened. Then look closely at the picture.

Can you tell your classmates what was happening?

Write down a sentence that tells you about this event.

Which parts of the story come before this event?

Which parts took place after the event?

Place your sentence where you think it fits in the story.

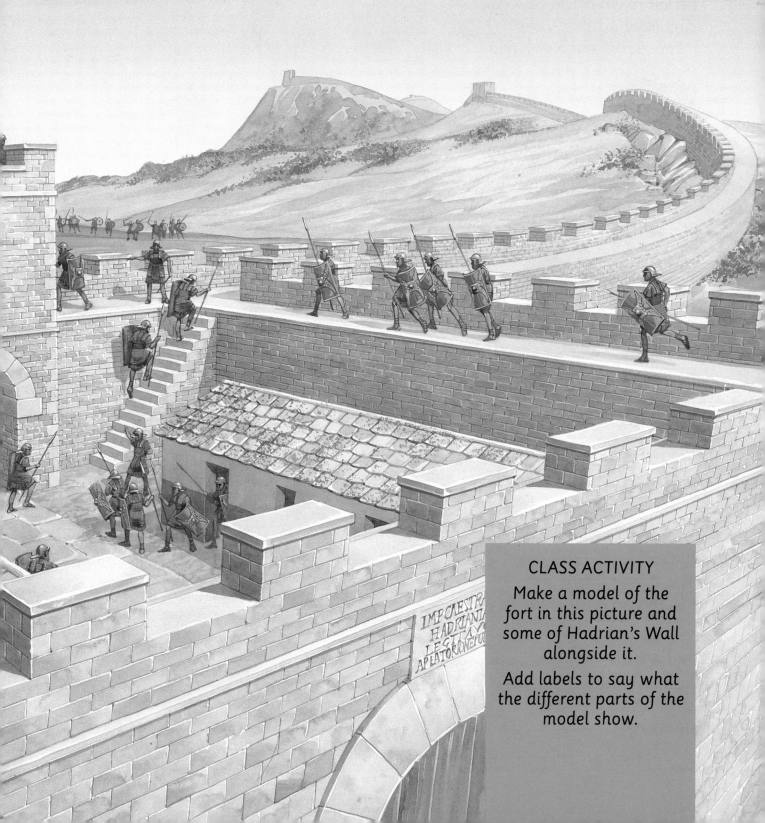

IMP CAESTRA
HADRIANI
LEG II AV
AP LATOMONEPO

CLASS ACTIVITY

Make a model of the fort in this picture and some of Hadrian's Wall alongside it.

Add labels to say what the different parts of the model show.

Along the Saxon shore

Clues help answer questions, such as: How did invaders come to Britain?

The next people to invade Britain were called Saxons, Angles and Jutes. They came across the North Sea from an area we now call Germany and Denmark.

Some of the first Saxon invaders came to steal from the homes of Britons and Romans.

We know there were signal towers along the coast of Britain to warn when the Saxons were coming.

And that the Romans used soldiers and ships, and built forts to protect the people of Britain against the invaders.

We also know about the boats that the Saxons used to come to Britain.

Archaeologists have found the remains of one boat. The remains were put together in a museum.

The boat is 23 metres long and 3 metres wide. It may have carried as many as 40 Saxons to British shores.

NORTH SEA

Hadrian's Wall
Northumbrians
York
Mercians
East Angles
West Stow · Sutton Hoo
Colchester
West Saxons
Kent
South Saxons

Imagine you were a Saxon invader. Use the picture and your own words to say why:

1. The journey to Britain was tiring.

2. The journey was uncomfortable.

3. The journey was dangerous.

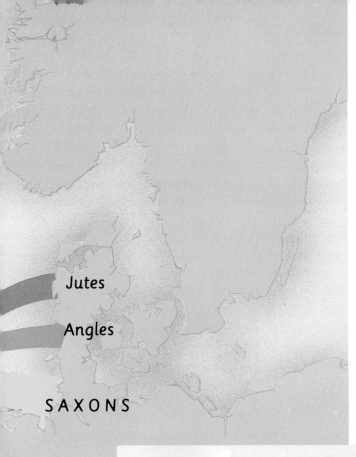

Jutes

Angles

SAXONS

Now use the photograph below to complete these sentences about the boat. Place one word from the blue box in each space.

The boat was made of _____ planks. It had no mast or _____, and was _____ to the sky. The Saxons must have _____ the boat over the sea. One man _____ the boat using a long _____ fixed to one side.

sail	paddle	steered
rowed	open	wooden

A.D.407 the last Roman
oops left Britain. Between
0.425 and A.D.450 many
ixons, Angles and Jutes
vaded Britain and settled
ere.

Treasure seekers

What happened when the Saxon invaders attacked the Britons and Romans?

Each of the pictures on these pages shows part of a story.

CLASS ACTIVITY

Work in groups to do this activity.

First say what is happening in each picture. Then, put the pictures in the order of when things happened.

Write a sentence to go with each picture.

Talk about why you think these Saxons had come to Britain.

Say whether their journey was successful or not.

Then see if your story is the <u>same</u> or <u>different</u> to those of other groups in your class.

A box and its secrets

This photograph shows an object that is now in a museum.

It was found in a country we now call Norway. But experts think that it was made in Britain.

What more can you find out about it?

About the object	Where to find the answer
What is its shape? What is it made of?	*Use the photograph on this page to answer these questions...*
Who made it? What do you know about its 'life'?	*The stories on pages 21 and 22 will help with these questions...*
Do you think there were many of these objects? Would it have been cheap or expensive to buy?	*Work out answers to these questions for yourself...*

Ranvaig owns me now.
She has scratched her name on my underside.
Ranvaig uses me as a box,
to hold coins and pieces of jewellery.
But I am no ordinary object.
I was made by skilled craftsmen,
and owned by Christian men.
At one time, I held the bones of a dead saint.
People travelled from far and wide to touch me.
In the hope the saint would forgive or help them in some way.
Then one day I was taken from my home, never to return.
I began a long journey over land and across the sea.
To the home of Ranvaig in a far-off place.
Now I lead a less important, but more private life!

CLASS ACTIVITY
Ranvaig's people lived in the lands now called Norway, Sweden and Denmark.

They visited the Mediterranean Sea and lands as far apart as Spain and Russia.

Use an atlas and see how far they travelled

A tale of terror

My name is Daniel.

I am a monk. A monk is a holy man who lives a simple life and helps people to become Christians.

I used to live in a monastery with other monks. The monastery was on an island off the coast of Britain.

I enjoyed my peaceful life of work, study and prayer.

Then our monastery was attacked by strangers from over the sea.

You will know that men of God carry no weapons.

But these strangers were not Christian men. They came with swords and axes.

Our crosses could not protect us from their swords and axes.

Some monks, like myself, escaped. Others were killed. And some were taken away as slaves.

Monastery buildings were set on fire. Everything of value was stolen: clothes, cups, candlesticks...

This belonged to a British Bishop. It was found in Sweden, which is one of the countries where Vikings lived.

Ranvaig's people and the strangers in Daniel's story are called Vikings. The Vikings first invaded Britain in A.D.787.

Use the story and picture on these pages to answer these WHY questions about them.

Why do the monks in the picture look afraid?

Why do you think the Vikings came to Britain?

Why did they attack monasteries like the one where Daniel lived?

Why did the Vikings steal crosses, when they were not Christian men?

Why do you think some monks, like Daniel, escaped?

Lost and found

The object below is only six centimetres long. But it is very valuable. Today we call it Alfred's Jewel.

Experts think it was made when the Saxon king called Alfred was alive.

It reads 'Alfred ordered me to be made' around the edge, And it was found about 300 years ago where Alfred had once hidden from Viking invaders.

Does all this prove that the jewel had once belonged to King Alfred, or not?

We are not really sure what Alfred's Jewel was. Some people think it was the handle of a pointer which was used to follow the lines of writing in a book.

We know that Alfred sent books and pointers to churches in his kingdom.

We also know that he later built a church where he had hidden from the Vikings.

Can you tell the story of Alfred's Jewel?

First, put these events in the order in which they happened:

1. Alfred's Jewel was found.
2. Alfred's Jewel was sent to a church.
3. Alfred became king.
4. Alfred's Jewel was placed in a museum.
5. Alfred's Jewel was lost.
6. Alfred's Jewel was made.

Then say:

How you think Alfred's Jewel got its name.

Why you think Alfred's Jewel was made.

Why Alfred's Jewel was found where it was.

Alfred ...
the Great?

This coin was made at the time of King Alfred. But we cannot be sure Alfred looked like this.

The picture strip tells you things we do know about him.

Some children have been doing a project on King Alfred.

Here are some of the things they said about him:

Tim said:

Alfred had ships built to fight against the Vikings.

Katy said:

Alfred ordered books to be written in English

Craig said:

Alfred was a handsome man.

Much of Alfred's early life was spent fighting the Vikings...

...at one time he was forced to hide in the marshes.

But later, Alfred won a great battle against the Vikings...

...the Vikings promised to leave Alfred's lands alone.

Alfred made his army stronger, in case other Vikings came...

...and he ordered ships to be built that could fight against them.

Alfred was interested in building... churches, schools and monasteries...

...and walls and ditches around towns, to keep the Vikings out.

Alfred was interested in learning...

...he had books written in English so that more people could read them.

Alfred kept law and order throughout his kingdom...

...he had a new book of laws written to protect his people.

Tina said:

When he was young Alfred had to hide from the Vikings.

Ali said:

People felt safe from the Vikings when Alfred was king.

Ben said:

Alfred was a great king!

Now use the picture strip to make two lists...

1. The names of the children who were talking about what they had read.

THESE ARE THE FACTS...

2. The names of the children who were saying what they were thinking.

THESE ARE POINTS OF VIEW...

Do you agree with Ben's point of view?

Use the picture strip to give one fact and one point of view of your own about Alfred the Great.

Where did they live?

Many of the Roman, Saxon and Viking invaders of Britain stayed here and became settlers.

The remaining pages of this book are about Saxon settlers.

Each double page will help you answer an important question about them; like, 'where did they live?'

We know where many Saxons were buried, for archaeologists have discovered their graves.

And old buildings still have Saxon parts, which is another clue.

Place names also help tell us where different groups of invaders settled.

You can find out how by using the map on this page.

This map shows part of West Sussex.

Sussex means 'the land of the South Saxons'.

Can you find the place called Ashurst on the map?

'Hurst' is a Saxon word. It means 'a clearing in a forest or wood'.

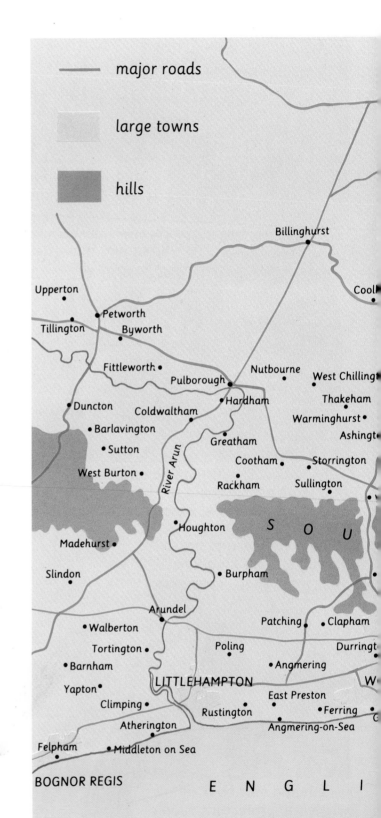

The blue box contains other Saxon words and their meanings.

BOURNE a stream

WORTH land with a fence around it

HAM a home, often near a river

TON a farm or small village

ING the people of a large family or tribe

Look for places on the map which include these words.

Make a list for each word.

Can you say why Saxon families liked to live:

1. in groups?

2. close to water?

3. near woodland?

CLASS ACTIVITY

Can you find out about Roman and Viking place names

ROMAN	VIKING
CASTER	BY
CHESTER	THWAITE
CESTER	THORPE

Do you know the names of any places which have these Roman or Viking words in them? You may use maps to help you if you wish.

Can you find out which invaders of Britain once settled near your home?

CRAWLEY

Warnham

HORSHAM

Slaugham

Nuthurst

HAYWARDS HEATH

Littleworth

Wineham

Twineham

BURGESS HILL

River Adur

Albourne Green

Ashurst

Henfield

Clayton

Poynings

Edburton Fulking

Keyning

Upper Beeding

D O W N S

West Blatchington

North Lancing

HOVE

BRIGHTON

Shoreham-by-Sea

South Lancing

C H A N N E L

0   5   10km

What were their buildings like?

Most Saxons lived in villages.

At West Stow, archaeologists found evidence of Saxon buildings.

There were stain marks which showed where posts had once stood.

The posts had helped make walls, and supported the roofs of buildings.

Why did the archaeologists find stain marks, and not the posts themselves?

Archaeologists used the marks to work out the size and shape of the buildings.

They then rebuilt some of them, as they think the buildings looked in Saxon times.

The picture below shows a Saxon *Hall*.

It is 8 metres long and 4 metres wide.

What can you say about its shape?
...its doors?   ...its walls?   ...its roof?

Every hall at West Stow was surrounded by five or six *houses*.

The one in the picture below is 6 metres long and 4¹/₂ metres wide.

These houses were:
1. where families went to sleep,
2. used to store things,
3. used as workshops.

How is your house different from the Saxon house at West Stow?

Copy out and complete this chart. Make a drawing in each of the spaces which remain.

HOUSES	THEN	NOW
Shape		
Doors		
Walls		
Roof		

Can you think of more things to compare then and now?

Add some more rows and drawings to your chart.

Why do you think the houses then are so different from houses now?

What did they believe in?

The first Saxon settlers of Britain were not Christians.

They were buried with their belongings beside them.

The Saxon believed their belongings would be useful in the life after death.

Alongside some bodies archaeologists have found silver and gold objects.

In the graves of poorer people simpler and cheaper things were found.

Saxon helmet found by archaeologists at Sutton Hoo ship burial site, near Ipswich

32

The objects on this page were found in a Saxon grave.

What are they?

Was the person who owned them rich or poor?

Why had they been placed where they were found?

Now look more closely at these objects.

One has a cross and the name SAUL engraved on it in Greek letters.

The other was engraved with the name PAUL, also in Greek letters.

The Bible tells the story of a man called Saul. He became a Christian and then changed his name to Paul.

"Maybe the spoons were a present for a rich man or king ... when he became a Christian?"

said Martin.

"But what if the king could not understand Greek? ... Perhaps the king just bought the spoons because he liked them?"

said Paula.

Whose point of view do you think is the best?

How were their churches built?

Many Saxons learnt about Jesus Christ from monks.

Monks could read and write, while most other Saxons could not. They needed monks to tell them the story of the Bible.

At first people listened to the monks while gathered around crosses in the open air. Then churches were built.

The first were wooden buildings.

Later some stone churches were built.

This picture imagines how a Saxon church was built.

Use the picture to check these sentences:

1. The church was the largest building in the village.

2. Its walls were built of stone.

3. The villagers did the work themselves.

4. The walls had no windows in them.

5. There was a tall tower at one end.

Which are true?

Which are not true?

Which are you not sure about?

Imagine you are the stone mason in charge of building the church.

You are telling the visitor in the red cloak about the jobs which:

1. have been done,

2. are being done at that time,

3. are still to be done.

Which of these jobs goes in each group?

Covering the roof

Putting up the scaffolding

Fetching stones from the quarry

The picture will help you to add more jobs to each list. Can you say why some jobs can be placed in more than one list?

The visitor has asked why the village needs a church. What should you say to answer him?

Which everyday jobs did they do?

Most Saxon settlers were farmers. They came to Britain to find new and better land for their families.

The two pictures below are from a very old calendar which shows people farming in Saxon times. The picture on this page is the one for March. The picture opposite is for August.

Look closely at both pictures. Then put these jobs in the order in which they were done in the farming year:

Carrying the corn to the cart.

Scattering the seed on the land.

Gathering the corn together.

Breaking up the soil in which the seed will grow.

Loading up the cart.

Cutting the corn which has grown in the fields.

Look at the picture for August below. At the left edge of the picture stands a person called the **reeve**.

Some children who looked at the picture had these ideas about the reeve...

Lee said:

The reeve is making sure all jobs are properly done...

Cathy said:

The reeve is blowing his horn for the meal break to start...

Tom said:

The reeve looks to be in charge of the other workers...

Louise said:

The reeve might not be popular with the other villagers...

Do you agree with these ideas?

Tick one box in each row of this chart. Then say why you ticked each box.

Have you any ideas of your own about the reeve?

Are these ideas facts or points of view?

IDEAS	YES	NO	NOT SURE
Tom			
Cathy			
Lee			
Louise			

What was it like to do these jobs?

Some jobs have changed since Saxon times and others have stayed the same.

The people in these pictures are visiting the rebuilt village of West Stow.

They are dressed in Saxon clothes.

They are acting out everyday jobs, as they were done in Saxon times.

Which different jobs can you see being done? Which objects were used to do these jobs? Make two lists.

Which of these jobs are still done today?

Write STILL DONE or NO LONGER DONE next to each job in your list.

Are the same objects used today as were used then?

Write STILL USED or NO LONGER USED next to each object.

Why have some jobs and objects changed, and others stayed the same?

CLASS ACTIVITY

Act out some of the everyday jobs in a Saxon village.

Each group should mime a different job and their classmates guess what they are doing. Later, words could be added.

Each group should say how difficult the work was. And what the reeve said about their efforts.

Group members could then talk to one another and to other groups about:

1. Jobs they enjoyed doing

2. Jobs they did not enjoy doing

The jobs were more fun to watch or mime than they would have been to do

said Robin.

Do you agree with Robin's point of view?

What was there to eat and drink?

Some things change, some things stay the same.

The Saxons often gathered in a hall to eat and drink together.

The picture on this page was drawn in Saxon times.

How many servers can you see?

What was each server carrying?

How many Saxons were being served?

What were these people doing?

Why do you think the servers were kneeling?

How different is the dining table in your home from the one in this picture?

Use the words in the blue box below to make two lists of:

1. things you can see on a dining table today,

2. things you can see in the Saxon picture.

table cloth   knife   fork

teapot   glass or cup   salt-cellar

Then use the picture and your own ideas to add more things to each list.

Underline those things you have included in both lists.

What do you think is the most important difference between eating and drinking *then* and eating and drinking *now*?

Stephen said:

The Saxons had a better and healthier diet than we do today.

Is this a *fact* or a *point of view*?

Do you agree with Stephen or not?

Now look at LIST A:

Some things the Saxons did eat and drink...

and LIST B:

Things the Saxons did not eat or drink...

Imagine a machine could take you back to Saxon times...

Which items from LIST A would you enjoy the most?

Which items from LIST B would you miss eating?

LIST A	LIST B
Bread	Potatoes
Beans	Tomatoes
Honey	Rice
Apples	Sugar
Fish	Tea
Cheese	Coffee
Milk	Crisps
Nuts	Bananas
Peas	Oranges
Smoked or salted meat	Tinned or frozen food

How did the Saxons entertain themselves?

An evening at home then was different from an evening at home now.

It was time to relax and have fun when the meal was over.

Some Saxons liked to sit and talk, and to tell jokes! Others liked to sing, or dance while musicians played.

Some Saxons played board games, or with dice. Others tried out riddles on their friends.

One person had to describe something they all knew about – like a ship or the fire – then the others had to guess what it was.

But the best moments were when storytellers told tales about great adventures. Like the story of Beowulf, a hero who killed two monsters and a dragon.

How different is an evening at home NOW from what it was like THEN?

Copy out and complete this chart:

ACTIVITY	THEN	NOW
Eating		
Talking		
Listening		
Watching		
Playing		
Reading		

Evenings at home were much more lively then!

You're joking... I much prefer what we do now...!

Do you agree with Diane or Michael?

Give reasons for your point of view.

CLASS ACTIVITY

Act out an evening's fun and games in Saxon times.

One group make up riddles about objects you can see in the picture on these pages.

Another group mime part of the story of Beowulf.

The third group work on a simple game for people to play.

Then show the whole event to visitors from another village.

How did the Saxons keep law and order?

Sometimes a Saxon king called together his Witan. The Witan was a group of wise men who advised the king.

It helped the king make the laws, and to see that they were obeyed.

There was no police force to deal with crimes then.

The punishments for crimes were often hard. You would be hanged if you tried to overthrow the king. Or if you gave

shelter to the king's enemies.

A thief might have his hand cut off.

What do you think happened to a liar?

What do you think:

the king and Witan were talking about in this picture?

the king had decided would happen?

Often a person who did wrong to someone else had to pay them a sum of money or fine. The amount to be paid depended on the victim's worth.

Each person had their own price, called WERGILD. Whose wergild do you think would have been the largest:

Daniel, the monk (page 22)?

The owner of the spoons (page 33)?

The reeve (page 37)?

Can you say why?

Each part of a person's body also had its own worth, or wergild.

Which do you think had the largest wergild:

A finger?

An eye?

A toe?

Can you say why?

One person is just as important as another... wergild was a stupid idea!

Do you agree or disagree with Emma's point of view?

What happened when a crime took place?

Ulf's chickens had been stolen. Some villagers said Oswald stole them. They said he was dishonest.

Oswald had to attend the village court. He said he was innocent. But Oswald did not have oath-helpers to swear he was not guilty. And so he had to face the ordeal.

A fire was started and a bar of iron placed upon it. Oswald had to carry the bar, fresh from the fire, for five paces. Afterwards his hands were bandaged.

That was yesterday.

Two days from now the bandages will be removed. If the burns on Oswald's hands are healing, he will be set free. If they are not, he is guilty and will be punished.

God will make clear the truth.

What do you think happened to Oswald?

Imagine your own ending to the story.

CLASS ACTIVITY

Make a play about a trial in the village court.

Ask your teacher to choose one of you to act as an imaginary person who has been accused of a crime.

Choose a suitable name and crime for the accused person.

Will the accused find oath-helpers and prevent a trial by ordeal?

What do you think about trial by ordeal?

Make up your own point of view......

Do your classmates agree or disagree with you?

Shelley has used this **INDEX** to find out about:

Real people	Imaginary people	Places	Important events	Everyday life	
	Ranvaig 21, 23	Mediterranean Sea 21 Monastery 22 Norway 20, 21 Russia 21 Spain 21 Sweden 21, 23	Viking attacks 20, 21, 22, 23		**1000 years ago**
Alfred 24, 25, 26, 27 Angles 16, 17 Christians 22, 23, 32, 33, 34 Jutes 16, 17 Monks 22, 23, 34 Reeve 37, 45 Witan 44	Beowulf 42, 43 Daniel 22, 23, 45 Oswald 46 Ulf 46	Denmark 16, 21 Germany 16 North Sea 16 Sutton Hoo 30, 31, 32, 33 West Stow 30, 31, 38, 39 West Sussex 28, 29	Saxon invasion 16, 17, 18, 19 Sutton Hoo ship burial 32, 33	Entertainment 42, 43 Food and drink 40, 41 Law and order 44, 45, 46, 47 Religion 32, 33, 34, 35 Work 36, 37, 38, 39	
Hadrian 12 Longinus 8	Lucius 12	Colchester 8, 10, 11	Hadrian's Wall 12, 13, 14, 15 Roman invasion 4, 5, 6, 7		
Boudicca 10, 11 Picts 13	Bran 4, 5, 6	A hill-fort 4, 5, 6, 7	Boudicca's revolt 10, 11		**2000 years ago**